The *Scottish Wild Food* Bible

The
Scottish Wild Food
Bible

Claire Macdonald

Illustrated by Bob Dewar

BIRLINN

For Mitch and Sam Partridge,
with love

First published in 2020 by
Birlinn Ltd
West Newington House
10 Newington Road
Edinburgh
EH9 1QS

www.birlinn.co.uk

ISBN: 978 1 78027 635 9

British Library Cataloguing-in-Publication Data
A catalogue record for this book is available on
request from the British Library

Designed and typeset by Mark Blackadder

Printed and bound by Bell & Bain Ltd, Glasgow

Contents

Introduction

I am, and always have been, in my mother's and grand-mother's footsteps, an ardent forager. I've just never thought to call it that.

Foraging is the most politically correct form of obtaining food growing in the wild. Extreme foragers, in my view, are those who post selfies on Instagram, clad in wetsuits and scuba diving gear, emerging from the sea clutching a bunch of seaweed. Or a single scallop. I some-times pick seaweed, but from the shore, not from the deeper sea. Yet foraging fascinates many people. We see this at first hand at Kinloch Lodge on Skye, where many of our guests ask to go on foraging expeditions, under the guidance of local expert Mitchell Partridge. People love to learn.

And there is the word 'pick', which differentiates those of us who have been foraging all our lives like our forefathers, from the present day 'foragers'. We've all – or very many of us have – been picking wild-growing foods for decades. Present-day foragers, though, don't pick, they tend to 'gather', or they 'harvest'.

Scotland and the whole of the United Kingdom is rich

in foods that are free, there for the picking. Autumn is the most prolific season – brambles, nuts, crabapples – but there is so much to pick, too, in the preceding months such as early nettles, sorrel and garlic. Elderflower gives us one of nature's exquisite flavours, usually encountered in cordial to be diluted with water, either still or sparkling. But elderflower can flavour sorbets and syllabubs, and the heads of tiny flowers are so good dipped in a tempura batter and briefly deep fried. Meadow-sweet is the same, giving a slightly sweeter and entirely different flavour. Wild blackcurrants grow in the hedges near where we live. Their leaves provide another exquisite flavour, and make my favourite of all water ices or sorbets.

Wild mushrooms – fungi – proliferate. If you don't have a genuine expert to accompany you on wild mush-room picking expeditions, get a copy of Roger Phillips' book, called simply *Mushrooms*. No one could ever mistake the edible from the inedible or downright poisonous when armed with this book, with its clear photographs and descriptions. But if you are picking without an expert, or without Roger Phillips with you in print, then never leave anything to chance. Always identify what you pick – particularly when it is from the fungus world. Some are edible but not worth the effort, but several are simply wonderful to eat – chanterelles, horns of plenty (although their name in French is disconcerting, *trompettes de la mort* . . .) and hedgehog mushrooms to name just three species.

The seashore also provides a multitude of wild growing food. I've already mentioned seaweed, and the sea also provides mussels, and clams and razor fish.

There are a few things to bear in mind when out foraging. It does seem obvious, but never pick fruit from a roadside where fumes might have affected fruit like brambles, and try to avoid picking from too low down, where dogs could have lifted their legs.

Finally, please forage sensibly. It is important only to pick and gather in places where there is a plentiful supply and never to exhaust supplies, as this denies other foragers the chance to collect. More crucially, stripping an area bare could mean using up a valuable food source that local wildlife depend on. Whilst the Land Reform (Scotland) Act 2003 allows everyone access to land for recreational and educational purposes, this right must be respected responsibly, and there are restrictions (for example, it is illegal to collect wild plants or fungi on a National Nature Reserve (NNR) or a Site of Special Scientific Interest (SSSI) without the express permission of Scottish Natural Heritage). If in doubt, there are numerous internet sources which have more detailed information.

Blackcurrant leaves

To many, blackcurrant leaves sound as if they must be cultivated, but this is not always the case. Round where we live on the Black Isle, the hedges contain black-currants growing wild, so I imagine that this is the same elsewhere. Most people think to use the berries, and I love them, but it is the leaves which yield one of the most exquisite of tastes – knocking even elderflower into second place. My favourite of all water ices – sorbets – is one made with blackcurrant leaves.

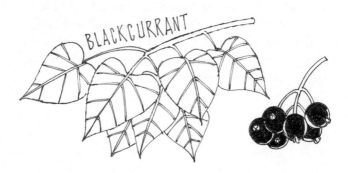

Blackcurrant leaf water ice

Serves 6

900ml (1½ pints) cold water
250g (9oz) granulated sugar
Pared rind of 1 lemon – use a sharp potato peeler to avoid any
    bitter white pith
2 good handfuls blackcurrant leaves

Put the water, sugar and pared lemon rind into a
saucepan over moderate heat. Stir until the sugar is
dissolved completely and you no longer feel any gritty
texture under your wooden spoon. Then raise the heat
beneath the pan and boil fast for 5 minutes. Take the pan
off the heat and plunge the blackcurrant leaves into the
very hot syrup. Leave to cool. When cold, strain through
a sieve and squeeze out the leaves. Discard the leaves. Put
the syrup into a solid polythene container and freeze.
After several hours, take the container from the freezer
and scrape into a food processor. Whizz. Refreeze.
Repeat this three more times.

If you follow this method, the water ice should be
spoonable from the freezer. If you own an ice cream
making machine, simply churn the syrup until it is
frozen!

Brambles

Wild brambles are as different to those which are cultivated and grown commercially as chalk is from cheese. Picking brambles involves a certain amount of effort – not the lovely walks to find them, not the carrying home of a bramble-filled basket or bucket, but the fact that the best brambles invariably grow just out of reach. But they are well worth the danger of teetering on the brink of a crevasse, toes clenched uselessly in wellies, to hook the branch and pick the berries. And scratched and stained hands are a proud badge of honour for the bramble picker. They go with the bramble season. They distinguish those of us who do pick from those who don't.

Brambles are entirely weather dependent. I follow their progress, from pretty flowers, to tiny green woody fruit, through red to a rich deep purply black. But what I dread is several days of continuous rain rendering 'my' brambles mushy on the briars.

My mother always used to maintain that following the first frost the brambles belonged to the Devil. But maybe that's only in Lancashire, where I come from!

Bramble jelly

Nothing beats homemade bramble jelly. I find any bought jelly is too sweet. I add lemon to enhance the flavour of the brambles. It is so good that I have known some people close to me to eat it spooned straight from the pot. But it is usually eaten spooned onto thickly buttered hot toast or scones.

2lb brambles, washed
1–2 good eating apples
Granulated or preserving sugar (see method for quantity)

Put scrupulously clean jam jars into a low-temperature oven to heat through.

Put your picked brambles into a large saucepan and add cold water to barely cover them. Depending on the amount of brambles, add 1 or 2 good eating apples, each washed and quartered – the apples help contribute pectin.

Bring the pan to a gentle simmer, and simmer gently for 20–25 minutes. The fruit should have turned soft. Cool the contents of the pan. Line a sieve with a J-cloth or a piece of muslin. Put the sieve on a large bowl or measuring jug and pour the contents of the pan into the lined sieve. You may need two jugs or bowls if you have picked a vast amount of brambles.

Leave the brambles to drip for several hours, then gently squeeze the contents of the cloth to get every last drop of juice from the cooked brambles.

Put a plate into the fridge to chill. This is for testing the jelly for a set. Measure the bramble juice into a clean saucepan. To each 600ml (1 pint) add 450g (1lb) granulated or preserving sugar and 1 tablespoon lemon juice.

Stir the contents of the pan over moderate heat, until every grain of sugar has dissolved. Only then let the liquid boil. Boil it fast, stirring occasionally, keeping a close eye not to let it overboil. After 10 minutes of really fast boiling, carefully draw the pan off the heat. Take the cold plate from the fridge and drip a dribble of hot liquid onto the plate. Leave for 2–3 minutes, then push the dribble with your fingertip. If it wrinkles, you have achieved a set, and the liquid will gel on cooling. If not, put the pan back on the heat and boil fast for a further 5 minutes, and test again. Always remember to take the pan off direct heat as you test.

Using a small jug, distribute the hot liquid between the heated jam jars. Cover each with a disc of waxed paper, and seal with cellophane. When cold, label and store the jars of bramble jelly in a cool place.

Bramble suedoise

A suedoise is a set puree of fruit or vegetables – in this
case brambles. You do have to sieve the pureed brambles
because their tiny woody seeds never pulverise in any
blender or food processor. This makes a perfect special
occasion pudding, with the suedoise turned out onto a
serving plate, and whipped vanilla-flavoured cream spread
all over it. The cream can then be studded with small
meringues if you like, or alternatively, serve the cream-
covered bramble suedoise with crisp, thin shortbread
biscuits.

Serves 6
750g (1½lb) brambles
175g (6oz) caster sugar
Finely grated rind and juice of 1 lemon
6 leaves of gelatine, soaked in cold water
450ml (¾ pint) double cream, whipped but not too stiffly with
    1 teaspoon vanilla extract and
    50g (2oz) caster sugar

Put the brambles, caster sugar, lemon rind and juice into
a saucepan on a moderate heat. Stir occasionally as the
sugar dissolves and the juice seeps from the brambles.
Cover the pan with its lid, and let the contents simmer
gently for 10 minutes once the sugar has dissolved.

    Tip the contents of the pan into a food processor

and whizz to a smooth puree. Put the contents of the processor into a sieve over a measuring jug. Push and work the bramble puree through the sieve mesh.

Spoon a small amount of seedless bramble puree into a small saucepan. Heat it, then lift the soaked gelatine leaves from the cold water and drop them into the hot puree. Stir to dissolve the gelatine, then mix this thoroughly through the rest of the pureed brambles. Pour into a Pyrex bowl. Leave to set in the fridge overnight.

To turn out, fill a basin with very hot water. Dip the bowl of set suedoise into the water for a count of 25, loosen the sides of the suedoise with a knife, then invert the bowl onto a serving plate and give it a good shake. If it doesn't dislodge the jelly, dip the bowl in the very hot water for a further few seconds and try again.

When the suedoise is turned out, use a palette knife to spread the entire surface with the sweetened vanilla-flavoured whipped cream. To serve, slice inwards towards to middle.

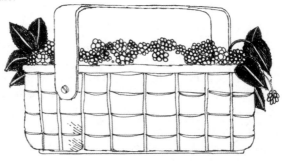

Bramble sauce

Perfect for eating with game, such as venison or roast duck.

_____

Serves 6
750g (1½lb) brambles
1 onion, skinned, halved and finely diced
600ml (1 pint) chicken stock – made from boiling water and a
      stock jelly or cube
1 sprig of thyme, about 3cm in length
2 level tablespoons granulated sugar
300ml (½ pint) red wine vinegar
1 teaspoon soft butter mixed very well with
      1 teaspoon plain flour
1 level teaspoon salt and about 10 grinds of black pepper

_____

Put the diced onion, brambles and sprig of thyme into a saucepan with the chicken stock. Bring the stock to a simmer, cover the pan with its lid and simmer gently for 15 minutes.

Meanwhile, in another saucepan heat the granulated sugar over moderate heat until it dissolves and forms an amber-coloured caramel. Shake the pan as the sugar dissolves, but don't be tempted to try to stir the caramel. Then add the red wine vinegar to the caramel in the pan – beware, it will whoosh as the liquid hits the hot caramel. Then stir gently, until the caramel dissolves in the vinegar. When dissolved, pour this into the pan

containing the brambles and onion. Stir in the butter and
flour mixture, stirring until the sauce boils and it thickens
slightly. Stir in the salt and pepper. Fish out and discard
the sprig of thyme. Taste, and add more salt or pepper if
you think it is needed.

This sauce can be made a day in advance, stored in
the fridge when cooled. Reheat before serving.

Bramble and lemon ice cream

Serves 6
450g (1lb) brambles
Finely grated rind and juice of 1 lemon
175g (6oz) granulated sugar
2 large egg whites
Pinch of salt
2 rounded tablespoons icing sugar, sieved
300ml (½ pint) double cream

Put the brambles, grated lemon rind and juices into a saucepan with the granulated sugar. Cover the pan with its lid, and cook on moderate heat, stirring occasionally, until the brambles are very soft. Take the pan off the heat, cool, then liquidise in a food processor, and sieve the resulting puree to get rid of the tiny woody seeds. Put the seedless puree into a bowl.

Whisk up the egg whites with the pinch of salt – which gives greater volume – and, when the whites are stiff, whisk in the sieved icing sugar, a spoonful at a time. Whisk until you have a stiff meringue. Cover the bowl of meringue with cling film to keep the air out.

Immediately, and using the meringue whisks (saves washing-up if you do it in this order), whip the double cream until thick but not stiff. Fold the bramble and lemon puree into the whipped cream, then fold the meringue mixture into the bramble cream. A metal whisk is the most efficient kitchen implement to do this quickly and thoroughly. Freeze in a solid plastic container. There is no need to beat this ice cream during its freezing time. It is fairly easy to serve straight from the freezer.

Bramble fudge crumble

The easiest and the best of crumbles – forget flour, buy
digestive biscuits (or gingernuts, or a combination of
both) and just combine them with butter and demerara
sugar for a crumble which is divine to eat! I serve this
with crème fraîche, but custard and/or double cream is
very good instead – or as well!

Serves 6
For the fruit filling:
750g (1½lb) brambles
120g (4oz) soft brown sugar
Finely grated rind and juice of 1 orange

Put the brambles, sugar, orange rind and juice into a
saucepan on a moderate heat. As the brambles heat, they
seep their juices. Cover the pan with its lid and cook for
20 minutes. Then tip the cooked brambles and their
juices into an ovenproof dish and leave to cool.

For the crumble:
120g (4oz) butter
120g (4oz) demerara sugar
220g (8oz) digestive biscuits pulverised into crumbs in a
    food processor

Melt the butter and heat the sugar together in a pan.
When the butter has melted, stir in the digestive crumbs.

SOFT
BROWN
SUGAR

demerara

Butter

Digestive

Mix thoroughly, then spoon this crumble mixture evenly
over the entire surface of the cooked brambles. Bake in a
hot oven, 200°C (400°F, Gas 6), for 15–20 minutes until
the crumble is buttery, dark golden and crisp on top.
Serve warm.

Bramble and lemon pudding

In this there is a very light sponge which forms as the pudding bakes, leaving the brambles sitting in a thick lemon curd-like sauce beneath. It is an amazingly useful and delicious pud. It freezes faultlessly when cooked and cooled, needing only 2–3 hours to thaw, and reheating gently before serving warm, with either crème fraîche or with sweet cream.

Serves 6
450g (1lb) brambles
75g (3oz) granulated or caster sugar

For the pudding:
150g (5oz) caster sugar
50g (2oz) soft butter
Finely grated rind of 1½ lemons and their juices
35g (1½ oz) self-raising flour, sieved
170ml (6fl oz) milk
4 large eggs, separated

Beat together the butter and sugar, then beat in the grated lemon rind and juice. Then beat in the yolks, one at a time. The mixture will almost invariably curdle, but don't worry about this, the pud turns out just fine! Mix in the sieved flour and the milk.

Whisk up the egg whites with a pinch of salt, which gives a greater volume, until stiff. Then fold quickly and thoroughly through the runny lemon mixture. Pour over the brambles. Put the dish into a roasting tin with almost-boiling water poured into the roasting tin, to come halfway up the sides of the pudding dish. Bake in a moderate heat, 180°C (350°F, Gas 4) for 45–50 minutes. Then take the roasting tin out of the oven and dust the surface of the pudding with a teaspoon of sieved icing sugar. Serve warm.

Crabapples

The whereabouts of crabapples are jealously and most protectively guarded. Crabapples are small, larger than a walnut but not by much, and as fruit they are bitter. But they make one of the best jellies to be eaten with all meats, especially game and chicken. Crabapples are the oldest wild variety of the domestic apple.

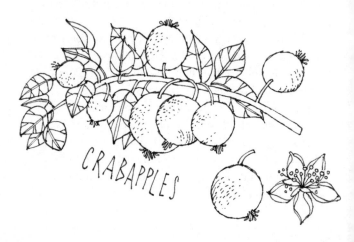

Crabapple jelly

10–12 crabapples, washed and quartered
Granulated sugar (see method for quantity)

Put the quartered crabapples into a large saucepan and just cover with water. Place over heat, bring the water to simmer, and cover the pan with its lid. Cook, gently simmering, for 35–40 minutes. The apple quarters should be very soft. Cool, and then pour the crabapples and cooking liquid into and through a large sieve lined with either a piece of muslin or a J-cloth. Leave the sieve to drain above the bowl or measuring jug – you may need two – for several hours.

Put a plate into the fridge to chill. Put 4 or 5 scrupulously clean jam jars into a low-temperature oven to heat through. Then discard the cloth and its contents, measure the liquid into a large saucepan, and add 450g (1lb) of granulated sugar per 600ml (1 pint) of crabapple liquid.

Over heat, stir until the sugar dissolves completely, then raise the heat beneath the pan and boil very fast, taking care not to let it over boil. After 10 minutes of fast boiling draw the pan off the heat, take the plate from the fridge and drip a dribble of crabapple liquid onto the cold plate. Leave for 4–5 minutes, then press the dribble

with your fingertip. If its surface wrinkles, your jelly will set. Divide between the heated jam jars, cover each with a disc of waxed paper, then seal with a cellophane disc. When cold, label the jars of crabapple jelly. Store them on shelves in a cool place, ideally a larder.

NB. If your first test for a set doesn't wrinkle on its surface, put the pan of crabapple liquid back on the heat and fast boil it for 5 minutes before drawing the pan off the heat and testing once more. The less boiling needed for a set, the brighter and fresher tasting the jelly will be.

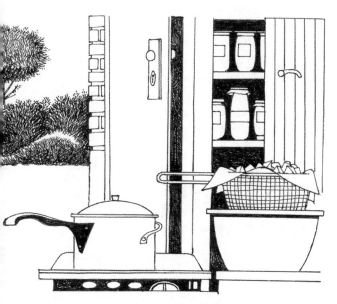

Dandelions

Dandelions, with their bright yellow flowers, grow prolifically in the wild. Yet it isn't the flowers which we eat, but the tender leaves, particularly those growing closest to the stems of the flowers. These leaves form the main part of a salad. But before I go further extolling the flavour of dandelion we should be reminded that in French dandelions are known as *pissenlit* – which means in polite terms that they are diuretic! As long as you don't tend to sleep like the proverbial log, you should be all right if you eat this delicious salad for supper.

DANDELION
LEAVES

Dandelion salad with golden croutons

Serves 6 as a starter, or an accompanying salad to a main course.

220g (8oz) young and tender dandelion leaves
50g (2oz) butter
1 tablespoon olive or rapeseed oil
3 slices of thickly sliced white bread, crusts removed and the bread
    cut into even-sized small squares, about ½ cm in size
Small bunch of chives, finely snipped with scissors

For the dressing:
2 tablespoons extra virgin or rapeseed oil
2 teaspoons lemon juice
1 teaspoon salt, about 10 grinds of black pepper
1 teaspoon caster sugar

Combine the dressing ingredients thoroughly.

Melt the butter and heat the tablespoon of oil in a sauté pan. Over moderate heat, fry the cubes of white bread, turning them over, until they are golden brown on all sides. Scoop them from the pan onto a double thickness of kitchen paper, to absorb excess butter and oil.

To serve, mix the dressing into the dandelion leaves in a serving bowl. Scatter the cooled croutons over the surface, and dust liberally with the snipped chives.

Elderflowers

From mid-June, depending on the weather and how cold or warm spring has been, our hedgerows and woods are filled with lace-like clusters of tiny white flowers at the end of vivid green-leaved branches of the elder tree. These are elderflowers, and they taste exquisite. I've experimented with freezing the heads to preserve their flavour for use in later months – don't bother! They lose all taste. But they can be wonderfully preserved in a cordial, where the flavour is every bit as delicious several months after being made. The elderflower season can end suddenly if we are cursed with high winds and rain, but all being well on the weather front, elderflowers should be available for 4–6 weeks.

ELDERFLOWERS

Elderflower cordial

Makes one bottle.

About 12 heads of elderflower
600ml (1 pint) cold water
Pared rind of 1 lemon – use a potato peeler to do this, to avoid
    any bitter white pith
175g (6oz) granulated sugar
Juice of 1 lemon

Put the water, pared lemon rind and granulated sugar
into a saucepan over moderate heat and stir until the
sugar dissolves completely. Then add the elderflower
heads, pushing them down into the liquid. Boil the
contents of the pan for 5 minutes. Take the pan off the
heat, add the lemon juice, and cool. Strain into a jug and
then store in a bottle until required. Store in a cool place,
ideally a larder. To drink, dilute with still or sparkling
water.

Elderflower and gooseberry jelly

The flavours of elderflower and gooseberry go as well together as do tomatoes and basil, or bacon and eggs. Elderflowers must have been created to be cooked with gooseberries. In this jelly, cooked gooseberries are beneath a gooseberry and elderflower clear jelly. Serve with whipped cream and crisp shortbread biscuits.

Serves 6
900g (2lb) gooseberries, topped and tailed, divided into two
    equal amounts
4 heads of elderflower
175g (6oz) sugar, either granulated or caster
150ml (¼ pint) water

For the jelly:
175g (6oz) sugar, either granulated or caster
10 heads of elderflower
900ml (1½ pints) water
Pared rind and juice of 1 lemon
8 leaves of gelatine, soaked in cold water for 10 minutes

Start by cooking the gooseberries for the compote to go beneath the jelly. Put half the gooseberries into a saucepan with the four heads of elderflower, the sugar and 150ml of cold water. Cover the pan with its lid and, over moderate heat, cook gently until the gooseberries are completely soft. Cool. When cold, fish out and discard the elderflower heads. Tip the gooseberries into a bowl – ideally a glass bowl for this recipe.

Meanwhile, put the other half of the gooseberries into a saucepan with the 10 heads of elderflower, water, sugar, lemon rind and juice. Over moderate heat, stir until the sugar has dissolved completely, then boil (but not furiously) for 5 minutes. Take the pan off the heat. Cool, then strain into a measuring jug. Put approximately 300ml of the liquid into a saucepan and heat it. When very hot, lift the soaked gelatine leaves from their water, drip off excess water and drop them into the hot liquid. Stir until the gelatine dissolves completely, which will be almost instantaneous. Stir this into the cold liquid in the measuring jug, chill until the liquid is just beginning to gel, then pour it over the gooseberries in the glass bowl. Leave to set fairly firmly before serving.

Elderflower fritters

Dusted lightly with caster or sieved icing sugar (I prefer caster) these elderflower fritters make a delicious finale to a meal. I allow three heads per person, but only two if a filling meal precedes the pudding course.

Serves 6
18 heads of elderflower

For the tempura batter:
2 large egg whites
125g (4oz) plain flour, sieved
150ml (¼ pint) sparkling water
Oil for deep frying – measure a depth of about 8cm / 3in in
    a saucepan
Caster sugar for sprinkling over the deep-fried elderflower heads

---

Whisk the egg whites until frothy and softly stiff. Then whisk in the sieved flour and, lastly, the sparkling water.

    Heat the oil in the pan, then dip three heads of elderflower in the batter and put them immediately into the hot oil for about 30 seconds. Lift them from the oil onto a baking tray lined with kitchen paper, and sprinkle each with caster sugar. Repeat until you have deep fried every elderflower head. Serve, to be eaten with fingers.

Fungi

This is such a potentially huge subject that I am going to restrict myself to my three favourites. These are chanterelles, horns of plenty and hedgehog mushrooms. In the introduction I made reference to the vital need – no exaggeration – to either pick wild mushrooms, known as fungi, with someone who really knows what they are doing, or buy yourself a copy of the truly excellent book *Mushrooms* by Roger Phillips. With that in hand, you can't go wrong. Without it, you may very easily kill yourself eating what you have picked, or maim yourself for life by mistaking one type for another.

Chanterelles grow widely throughout Scotland and the rest of the British Isles, usually under beech trees and often growing through mossy surfaces. They are apricot coloured, and I have often read that they smell of apricots. Not to me they don't! They do have a lovely, clean fragrance to them, but any resemblance to apricots stops with their colour.

In these recipes, all types of fungi are interchangeable. Some readers may miss any reference to ceps, but this is because I dislike them intensely and just couldn't recommend anyone eating them when I find them so abhorrent. I imagine that eating sliced slugs would be exactly how sliced cooked ceps are to me. Do you see what I mean?!

Chanterelle

Horn of Plenty

Hedgehog Mushroom

CHEEK

A SLUG

Chanterelle and leek soup

This is a light soup with a delicious flavour.

Serves 6

Approximately 450g (1lb) chanterelles – or any other variety of
    fungi – each wiped clean and any bits of grass, or moss picked
    off and discarded

50g (2oz) butter

1 onion, skinned, halved and finely diced

4 medium leeks, each trimmed at either end and then each leek
    finely sliced

½ teaspoon medium curry powder

1.2 litres (2 pints) chicken stock – this can be made using boiling water
    and 2 chicken stock jellies (or use vegetable stock if you prefer)

1 level teaspoon salt, about 10 grinds of black pepper

2 tablespoons finely chopped parsley

Chop the fungi neatly. Heat the butter in a large
saucepan and fry the diced onion for a couple of
minutes. Then add the sliced leeks and cook over
moderate heat – the leeks shouldn't turn colour – for
8–10 minutes, until they are very soft. Add the curry
powder and the chopped fungi, and stir well into the soft
leeks and onion. Cook for 2–3 minutes before adding the
stock, then the salt and pepper. Bring the liquid to
simmering point, half cover the pan with its lid, and
simmer gently for about 15 minutes. Just before serving,
stir the finely chopped parsley through the soup.

Wild mushroom linguine

You can use a mixture of wild mushrooms for this, or just one sort, depending on what you pick.

Serves 6

2 onions, each skinned, halved and finely diced
3 tablespoons olive oil
500g (1lb) wild mushrooms, chopped into fairly even bits
2 more tablespoons olive oil
1 level teaspoon salt
12–15 grinds of black pepper
1 heaped tablespoon finely chopped parsley
750g (1½lb) linguine (or spaghetti or fettucine, if you prefer) boiled
    in salted water until it retains a bite, about 4–5 minutes'
    cooking. Retain 150ml (approx.) of the cooking liquor. Drain
    the pasta then toss it in
2 tablespoons olive oil

Start by lining a baking tray with parchment and put the chopped mushrooms on this. Mix 2 tablespoons of olive oil thoroughly through the chopped mushrooms, sprinkle the salt over, and grind the black pepper. Roast in a hot oven at 200°C (400°F, Gas 6) for 30 minutes.

Meanwhile, heat the 3 tablespoons of olive oil in a wide sauté pan and fry the diced onions, stirring occasionally, on a moderately high heat, for about 5 minutes.

As you are doing this, cook the pasta.

Put the roasted mushrooms into the sauté pan with the onions, tip in the drained pasta and add the 150ml of the pasta cooking liquid. Mix everything together well over moderate heat, and just before dividing between six warmed plates, stir the finely chopped parsley thoroughly through the pasta and roasted mushrooms.

Wild mushroom sauce

This is so good with any plainly cooked – grilled or baked – fish or chicken. The sauce adds a touch of luxury.

OLIVE
OIL

fruity

SAUVIGNON
BLANC

CREAM

DOUBLE

Chicken
Stock

SALT

NUTMEG

Serves 6

2 shallots, each skinned, halved lengthways and finely diced
450ml (¾ pint) chicken stock
300ml (12fl oz) dry and fruity white wine (I like to use a sauvignon blanc)
450g (1lb) wild mushrooms, each wiped and picked free from bits of moss, grass or leaves
2 tablespoons olive or rapeseed oil
1 teaspoon salt, about 10–15 grinds of black pepper
300ml (½ pint) double cream
A grating of nutmeg

Chop the wild mushrooms neatly. To cook the mushrooms, line a baking tray with a sheet of parchment. Put the chopped wild mushrooms onto this and add the oil, salt and black pepper. With your hands, mix all together thoroughly, spreading out the mushrooms. Roast in a hot oven at 200°C (400°F, Gas 6) for 30 minutes.

Meanwhile, put the diced shallots, stock and white wine into a saucepan and simmer until the liquid has reduced by three quarters in amount. Add the roasted mushrooms to the contents of the pan, and stir in the double cream. Simmer gently until the sauce is the consistency you like – it should coat the back of a spoon. By using double cream the fat content thickens as it simmers. Taste, and add more salt and pepper if you think it is needed. Serve.

Wild mushrooms with garlic, parsley and thyme

I like to make this and serve it on buttered toasted sourdough bread. Unlike other recipes, where the serving is for six, please note that this recipe serves two. Just double up the amounts for every extra two people.

Serves 2

1 fat clove of garlic, peeled and very finely diced
4 tablespoons extra virgin olive oil
375g (¾lb) wild mushrooms, each wiped and bits of grass, moss or leaves picked off
Level tablespoon parsley, finely chopped
About half a teaspoon thyme leaves, stripped from their woody stems
1 level teaspoon salt, about 10 grinds of black pepper
Toasted bread, well buttered, for serving

Heat the oil in a frying pan – and please forget anything you may have read about extra virgin olive oil not being good to cook with, as these claims have been discounted scientifically.

Chop the wild mushrooms neatly. Fry the diced garlic over moderate heat for a couple of minutes, but take care not to let the garlic brown. Then add the chopped mushrooms, salt and black pepper, and mix thoroughly through the garlic oil. Add the thyme – but not the chopped parsley yet – and half cover the pan with its lid. Cook gently, stirring occasionally, for 8–10 minutes, then stir in the finely chopped parsley.

Divide evenly between the slices of buttered toast and eat.

Wild garlic

You smell wild garlic before you see it. During the spring months of March and April, the woods throughout Scotland are filled with the tiny white-flowered wild garlic. If you are new to it, don't think that wild garlic is much the same as the fat bulbs of garlic we buy in the shops. It isn't. Wild garlic has a tiny bulb root, but the compensation for lack of root substance is that we can use the leaves in a number of ways and recipes. Wild garlic isn't a strong taste, although its fragrance would make you think that it is!

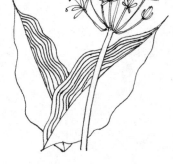

Wild garlic and potato soup

Serves 6
3 tablespoons rapeseed or olive oil
2 medium onions, peeled, halved and chopped
450g (1lb) potatoes, peeled and chopped
1.2 litres (2 pints) chicken or vegetable stock
2 rounded tablespoons finely chopped wild garlic leaves
2 teaspoons lemon juice
1 teaspoon salt, about 10 grinds of black pepper

Heat the oil in a saucepan and fry the chopped onions over moderate heat for about 5 minutes until they are transparent, but not changing colour. Stir occasionally. Then add the chopped potatoes to the pan, stir well, and continue to cook for a further 5 minutes, stirring from time to time. Now add the stock. Bring the liquid to a gentle simmer. Half cover the pan with its lid, and simmer gently until a chunk of potato squishes against the side of the pan with your wooden spoon, about 20–25 minutes.

Stir in the lemon juice, salt and black pepper and whizz, using a hand-held blender, to a smooth texture. Stir in the chopped wild garlic leaves, taste, and add more salt and/or pepper if you think it is needed. Reheat to serve.

Wild garlic dumplings

These can be added to any casseroled meat or game.
They are pushed down among the meat and vegetables
to cook for the final 30 minutes of the casserole cooking
time. They make a welcome alternative to potatoes or
rice, and are so easy to make and to cook.

Makes 8 ping-pong-ball-sized or 12 walnut-sized
dumplings.

220g (8oz) self-raising flour, sieved with
    1 teaspoon salt and about 10 grinds of black pepper
120g (4oz) suet – I buy the vegetarian suet
Finely grated rind of 1 lemon
2 tablespoons finely chopped wild garlic leaves
Cold water

Put the sieved seasoned flour, suet and lemon rind into a
mixing bowl. Mix in small amounts of cold water until
you have a dough. Mix in the chopped wild garlic leaves.
With floured hands, form the dough into 12 even-sized
balls. Drop them into your stew or casserole, pushing
them down gently. Cover the casserole with its lid and
cook from simmering for 25–30 minutes.

Wild garlic salad dressing

This dressing enhances any leaf salad. It is also very good on a steamed vegetable such as broccoli.

300ml (½ pint) extra virgin olive oil
2–3 tablespoons lemon juice (taste after adding 2 tablespoons, and the third is up to you)
1 rounded teaspoon salt, about 15 grinds of black pepper
1 level teaspoon caster sugar
1 rounded tablespoon of finely chopped wild garlic leaves

Put all the ingredients into a screw-topped jar and shake vigorously. Keep the jar in the fridge until 30 minutes before using, and shake well before pouring over the salad or steamed vegetables.

Wild garlic, cannellini bean and vegetable ragout

This is a simple, delicious and extremely nutritious lunch or supper dish. And its calorific content is low, too, which is a constant consideration for many of us!

Serves 6

3 tablespoons olive or rapeseed oil
2 medium onions, white if possible, peeled, halved and finely sliced
3 leeks, each trimmed at either end and very finely sliced
Thumb-length piece of ginger, skin pared off and the ginger chopped finely
3 sticks of celery, trimmed at either end and finely sliced
3 carrots, peeled and trimmed at either end and finely sliced
220g (8oz) broccoli, cut into 2cm pieces, florets, stalks and all
220g (8oz) sugarsnap peas, each sliced into 3
2 tins of chopped tomatoes
Finely grated rind of 1 lemon
220g (8oz) cannellini beans, tinned or from a jar
1 teaspoon salt, about 15 grinds of black pepper, half a teaspoon dried chilli flakes (optional)
2–3 tablespoons finely sliced wild garlic leaves, added 5 minutes before serving

---

Heat the oil in a wide-based saucepan, and fry the finely sliced onions, leeks, ginger and celery, stirring occasionally, for about 10 minutes over moderate heat. The vegetables should soften but not turn colour. Then stir in the finely sliced carrots, broccoli and the tinned tomatoes. Half cover the pan with its lid and simmer the contents gently until the carrots are soft when stuck with a fork, about 20–25 minutes. Then stir in the sliced sugarsnap peas, grated lemon rind, cannellini beans, salt, black pepper and chilli flakes if you are using them. Simmer gently for a further 10–15 minutes. Five minutes before serving, stir in the finely sliced wild garlic leaves.

Beetroot, apple and wild garlic coleslaw

This is so much nicer to eat than the usual carrot and cabbage slaw. Raw beetroot is a softer root than carrot, and for me, it has a delicious flavour. It can be a first course or it can be a very useful salad to accompany a main course. And it looks so pretty, too.

Serves 6

900g (2lb) raw beetroot, weighed before peeling
4 eating apples, peeled, cored and coarsely grated and mixed with
    2 tablespoons lemon juice, to help prevent discolouring

For the dressing:

4 tablespoons crème fraîche or Greek yogurt, whichever you
    prefer (I love both)
1 rounded teaspoon horseradish sauce
1 teaspoon salt, about 10 grinds of black pepper
2 tablespoons finely sliced wild garlic leaves

Cut the ends off the beetroot, and peel them – this takes no time at all using a good potato peeler. Don't worry about staining your hand purple as this washes off easily. Using a coarse grater, grate each beetroot into a bowl. Add the grated apples to the beetroot.

Mix together the ingredients for the dressing, and mix the dressing thoroughly through the beetroot and apples. Serve either in a bowl or on an ashet.

Wild garlic pâté

This can be spread on small oatcakes and served with smoked salmon, or it can be used as a dip for thin sticks of raw vegetables.

400g (just less than 1lb) cream cheese – I use full-fat Philadelphia
1 teaspoon salt, about 10 grinds of black pepper
1 level tablespoon of paprika
Finely grated rind of ½ lemon
2 tablespoons very finely sliced wild garlic leaves

Beat the cream cheese, then add the rest of the ingredients. Pile into a bowl and store, the bowl covered, in the fridge until 25–30 minutes before serving.

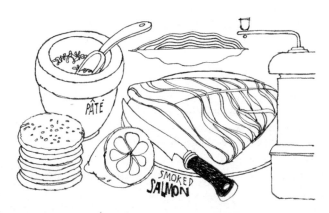

Cheese, white wine and wild garlic soup

This soup is unusual and delicious. Originally the idea for this soup comes from Germany, but I prefer my version in which I use potato to thicken the soup rather than flour.

Serves 6

2 leeks, trimmed at either end and then very finely sliced

450g (1lb) potatoes (I invariably buy the Rooster variety for all cooking), peeled and chopped small – no bigger than 1cm in size

3 tablespoons olive or rapeseed oil

2 rounded teaspoons granulated sugar

150ml (¼ pint) dry white wine

900ml (1½ pints) vegetable or chicken stock

2 bay leaves

A sprig of thyme about thumb length (or half a teaspoon dried thyme leaves)

2 cloves of garlic, skinned

Pared strip of lemon rind – use a potato peeler to do this, which avoids any bitter white pith

175g (6oz) good hard cheese, either a Mull cheddar, or Lancashire cheese, coarsely grated

Salt, to taste, about 15 grinds of black pepper

2 tablespoons finely sliced wild garlic leaves

Heat the oil in a wide-based saucepan and cook the finely sliced leeks over moderate heat until soft, about

5–7 minutes. The leeks should not turn colour. Add the diced potatoes to the leeks, and cook, stirring occasionally, for 5 minutes.

Meanwhile, put the sugar into a small saucepan over heat. Shake the pan from time to time as the sugar gradually dissolves into a molten amber caramel. Then pour the white wine into the caramel, gently shake the pan as the caramel melts into the wine. Simmer for 2 minutes, then pour this into the potatoes and leeks. Add the stock, bay leaves, thyme, garlic cloves and strip of lemon rind. Bring the stock to simmer, half cover the pan with its lid and simmer very gently for 25 minutes.

Take the pan off the heat and fish out and discard the lemon rind, bay leaves and thyme. Stir in the grated cheese and whizz, using a hand-held blender, until smooth. Taste, add salt as you think it is needed, and stir in the black pepper and finely sliced wild garlic leaves. Serve.

NB. If you need to reheat the soup, do this gently and don't let the soup come anywhere close to boiling.

Hazelnuts

As with other foods in this book, of course, you can buy hazelnuts all year round. And they are fairly expensive. But during late September and October we can pick our own hazelnuts.

My love for eating nuts borders on addiction. Quite possibly I was a dormouse in a previous life. But above all the varieties of nut, if I had to pick out a favourite, it would be hazelnuts. Toasted hazelnuts have a wonderful flavour, and one which not only combines but enhances so very well that of many other foods, both savoury – fish, chicken and meat – and sweet, including many fruits and chocolate.

Perhaps surprisingly, storing nuts in an airtight container isn't nearly as successful a method of preserving them as freezing the nuts.

One big consolation to my addiction is that nuts are extremely nutritious. They should form a part of our daily diet. For me, this is no hardship but is actively a joy!

Hazelnut, shallot and lime stuffing

This is so good to stuff a chicken, but it can also be used to coat filleted fish which is then baked. This quantity makes enough to stuff a chicken weighing 1.5 kg (3lb) or to coat six pieces of filleted fish.

175g (6oz) hazelnuts, dry fried to toast them until they are light beige in colour. Cool, then cover the pan containing the nuts with cling film, and bash them to coarse crumbs.
4 tablespoons olive or rapeseed oil
4 banana shallots, each peeled, halved lengthways and finely diced
1 stick of celery, finely sliced
1 teaspoon salt, about 12–15 grinds of black pepper
175g (6oz) porridge oats
2 tablespoons finely chopped parsley
Finely grated rind of 2 limes

Heat the oil in a wide sauté or deep frying pan. Fry the finely chopped shallots and sliced celery over moderate heat for 7–10 minutes, stirring occasionally. The shallots should turn transparent, but not colour. Scoop the contents of the pan into a bowl, and add the porridge oats, salt and pepper. Cook over moderate heat, stirring occasionally, for about 5 minutes to toast the oatmeal. Then mix the softened shallots and celery back into the pan with the seasoned porridge oats. Mix in the roasted hazelnut crumbs and the finely grated lemon rind. Stuff into either a chicken, or two pheasants, or use to cover filleted fish.

Hazelnut and brown sugar meringues

Serves 6, allowing 1 meringue (2 halves) per person.

6 large egg whites
175g (6oz) granulated sugar
175g (6oz) demerara sugar
175g (6oz) toasted hazelnuts – to toast, dry fry them in a wide pan,
    shake the pan occasionally, for as many minutes as it takes to
    colour the hazelnuts deep beige. Cool, then cover the pan with
    cling film and bash the nuts to small chunks.

Whisk up the whites with a pinch of salt – which gives greater volume – until stiff but still glossy. Whisk in the combined sugars, a spoonful at a time. When you have a stiff meringue, stop whisking and add the cold bashed hazelnuts. Fold twice, then either pipe 12 even-sized meringues with a very wide nozzle or spoon them onto a parchment-lined baking tray. Bake in a low-temperature oven at 150°C (300°F, Gas 2) for 2½ to 3 hours. Take them out of the oven, and the meringues should lift easily from the paper. When cold, store in an airtight container.

Sandwich the meringues together in pairs, with stiffly whipped vanilla-flavoured double cream.

Hazelnut and apple cake

In this cake, the apples are pureed and mixed with whipped cream to fill the hazelnut cake. It can be eaten either with a cup of tea, or as a pudding.

Serves 6–8

175g (6oz) hazelnuts, dry fried in sauté pan to toast. Cool,
    then whizz in a food processor to coarse crumb texture
175g (6oz) soft butter
175g (6oz) caster sugar
3 large eggs
75g (3oz) self-raising flour, sieved
1 teaspoon vanilla extract

Beat together the butter and sugar until fluffy. Beat in the eggs, one at a time. Add the sieved flour and pulverised toasted hazelnuts, and the vanilla. Mix thoroughly.

Butter two non-stick cake tins about 16cm / 8in diameter and line the base of each with a disc of baking parchment. Divide the cake mixture evenly between the tins, smooth the surfaces, and bake in a moderate oven at 180°C (350°F, Gas 4) for 25 minutes. Test by sticking a knife into the centre of one cake – it should emerge clean. The cakes are cooked when they slightly pull away from the sides of their tins. Cool in the tins for 5 minutes before turning out to cool on a wire rack.

Filling:
2 cooking apples, quartered, peeled, cored and chopped into a
    saucepan
Finely grated rind and juice of 1 orange
1 rounded tablespoon soft brown sugar

Cover the pan with its lid and cook gently on moderate
heat until the apples fall to a soft mush. Beat with a
wooden spoon. Cool.

Fold the cooled puree into:
300ml (½ pint) double cream, whipped fairly stiffly with
1 dessertspoonful of icing sugar

To assemble, put one hazelnut cake onto a serving plate.
Spread with the apple cream. Cover with the second
cake, dust the surface with a spoonful of sieved icing
sugar.

Hazelnut crumble with pears and ginger

My favourite variety of pear is Conference. For this, choose pears which are fairly hard, not yet ripe. They cook so much better.

Serves 6

8 pears, each quartered, cored and peeled and put into a
   saucepan with
75g (3oz) soft brown sugar, light or dark
5–6 chunks of stem ginger, drained of preserving syrup and diced
Juice of 1 orange

Put the pan on a moderate heat and cook the pears until soft. Tip into an ovenproof dish.

For the crumble:

75g (3oz) butter
175g (6oz) gingernut biscuits, whizzed to fine crumbs in a
   food processor
75g (3oz) hazelnuts, bashed into chunks
75g (3oz) demerara sugar

Melt the butter in a saucepan and fry the chunks of hazelnut for 2–3 minutes. Then stir in the demerara sugar and the gingernut crumbs. Mix very thoroughly, then spoon this over the cooked pears. Smooth even. Bake in a hot oven at 200°C (400°F, Gas 6) for 20–25 minutes, until the crumble top is crisp when tapped with a metal spoon.

Serve this pudding warm, with either crème fraîche – my choice – or with pouring or whipped cream.

Hazelnut biscuits

Makes about 20.

75g (3oz) hazelnuts, dry fried to toast them, cooled, then bashed
    gently to break them into coarse crumbs
75g (3oz) softened butter
75g (3oz) sieved icing sugar
75g (3oz) sieved cornflour
1 teaspoon vanilla extract

Beat together the butter and icing sugar, then work in
the hazelnuts, cornflour and the vanilla. Line a baking
tray with parchment. Divide the biscuit mixture into
small even-sized blobs about the size of a walnut. Space
them evenly, and very gently press each down. Bake in
a moderate oven at 180°C (350°F, Gas 4) and check after
20 minutes – the biscuits will have spread and should
look golden. Take the tray out of the oven and cool.
When the biscuits are cold, store them in an airtight tin.

NB. You can, if you like, melt dark chocolate and use it
to coat the top of each biscuit. You need approximately
75g (3oz) dark chocolate to melt.

Meadowsweet

Like elderflower, meadowsweet consists of tiny lacy white flowers. But it tastes different to elderflower, not surprisingly. I use meadowsweet to flavour a syrup, which can then be made into a sorbet, or used with lemon in a syllabub, which is very good served over marinated wild strawberries.

Meadowsweet syrup

3 good handfuls of meadowsweet flowers
900ml (1½ pints) cold water
220g (8oz) granulated sugar
Juice and pared rind of 1 lemon – I use a potato peeler to do this,
    which avoids any bitter white pith

Put the water, granulated sugar and pared lemon rind
into a saucepan over moderate heat. Stir until every grain
of sugar has dissolved. Then boil the syrup fast for 5
minutes, the pan uncovered. Take the pan off the heat,
plunge the meadowsweet flowers into the very hot
syrup, and leave to cool. Then strain the cold syrup and
stir in the juice of the lemon.

Meadowsweet sorbet

Serves 6
1 batch of meadowsweet syrup

Freeze the syrup in a solid plastic container, box or bowl. When frozen, chip the iced syrup into a food processor and whizz until smooth. Return the whizzed syrup to the container and freeze.

Repeat this three times, at your convenience, over the course of several days. The sorbet becomes easier to spoon into the food processor with each session of whizzing. After the fourth and final session you should have a sorbet which is spoonable from the freezer.

Meadowsweet and lemon curd

Makes 1 pot.

Finely grated rind and juice of 2 lemons
1 large egg beaten with 2 large egg yolks
120g (4oz) granulated sugar
120g (4oz) butter, cut into small bits
A handful of meadowsweet flowers

Put all ingredients except the meadowsweet flowers into
a heatproof bowl, and put the bowl over a saucepan
containing simmering water. Stir, using a wire whisk,
until the butter is melted and the sugar dissolved. At this
point add the meadowsweet flowers. Then stir, using a
wooden spoon now, until the curd thickens enough to
coat the back of your wooden spoon to a depth of about
the same thickness as the spoon itself. Take the pan off
the heat, and sieve the curd through a fine meshed sieve.
You need to do this in order to have
smooth textured curd and to get rid
of the meadowsweet flowers having
obtained their flavour. Put the smooth
curd into a warmed jar, then cool,
cover, and label. Store in the fridge
once cooled, for up to a week.

Meadowsweet and lemon syllabub with wild strawberries

This is good eaten on its own, served with crisp, thin shortbread biscuits. But it is also very good spooned over a small amount of wild strawberries. I never can pick more than a small amount of wild strawberries, so I do need a recipe to be able to share them. The alternative is to eat them as I pick ...

Serves 6

450ml (¾ pint) double cream, whipped until fairly stiff with finely grated rind of 1 lemon and its juice
1 pot of meadowsweet lemon curd

Stir the lemon curd into the lemon whipped cream. Divide evenly between six glasses, spooned over the wild strawberries in the base of each glass. Garnish with a sprig of wild strawberry leaves, but please, NOT with a sprig of mint.

Wild mint

Generally speaking, wild mint is the variety known as spearmint, which has long, pointy leaves. Having access to handfuls of mint makes for a luxury while making sauces such as a salsa verde, which is good with everything I can think of – meat, fish or fowl and most vegetables too. Salsa verde keeps in the fridge, in a covered container, for up to a week. And mint sauce is another simple sauce, good with all lamb dishes. But I use a minimum amount of vinegar in my mint sauce – too often mint sauce is harshly redolent of vinegar which knocks all taste of mint, never mind the lamb it is supposed to enhance, on the head. All you taste is vinegar!

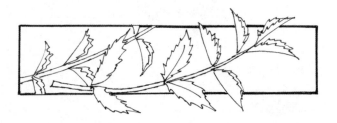

Salsa verde

2 good handfuls of mint leaves – discard any tough stalks
1 handful of parsley, either curly or flat leaf
2 cloves of garlic, each peeled and chopped
2 anchovy fillets, drained of their oil
About 10 grinds of black pepper – no need for salt as the anchovies
    provide sufficient saltiness for most palates
Finely grated rind of 1 lemon, and juice of half the lemon
300ml (½ pint) extra virgin olive oil

Put the mint, parsley, chopped garlic and anchovies into a
food processor and whizz, adding the olive oil and black
pepper. Whizz in the lemon rind and juice.

    Scrape from the processor into a bowl, cover and
keep in the fridge. As the salsa verde sits, the oil comes to
the surface. Before serving, stir well to mix the olive oil
into the rest of the salsa.

Mint sauce

Mint sauce is such a British classic, yet too often it is harsh with vinegar, almost eye-wateringly so. This version isn't.

---

3 handfuls of mint leaves
1 rounded teaspoon salt
2 level teaspoons caster sugar
About 12–15 grinds of black pepper
Juice and finely grated rind of 1 lemon
3 teaspoons white wine vinegar and 4 tablespoons cold water

On a large board and using a large and very sharp knife, finely chop the mint leaves with the salt and finely grated lemon rind. You get a much better result if you chop this by hand than if you pulverise in a food processor.

Meanwhile, put the lemon juice, wine vinegar and water into a saucepan with the caster sugar. Over moderate heat, stir until the sugar dissolves completely, then boil for 1 minute. Mix this liquid, still hot, and the finely chopped mint, salt and lemon rind together well. Serve in a small bowl so your guests can help themselves to a teaspoonful with their roast lamb.

Nettles

Nettles, when picked young, are delicious. Young nettles are brighter in colour than their aged, darker green counterparts, which tend to be more fibrous in texture. You need a good thick pair of gloves to pick them, and pick a basket full because, like spinach, when nettles cook they wilt down. My reference in the introduction to being wary as to where you pick wild foods applies very much when nettle-picking. Just be aware that dogs may have peed on them, and pick from the back of the nettles.

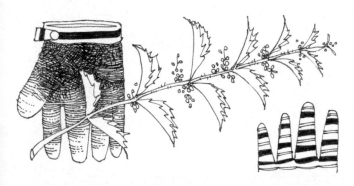

Nettle gnudi with hazelnut garlic butter

Gnudi are soft poached dumplings. They are so easy to make, and so delicious to eat. I first made them using spinach, but they are delicious made with nettles instead. If you wish, you can add sorrel to the nettles.

Serves 6

500g (1lb) nettles, or a mix of nettles and sorrel
250g (9oz) ricotta
100g (4oz) semolina flour, or plain flour
2 egg yolks
100g (4oz) parmesan cheese, grated
½ teaspoon salt, about 12 grinds of black pepper

For the nuts:

75g (3oz) butter
50g (2oz) hazelnuts, bashed to chunks using the end of a
    rolling pin
2 fat cloves of garlic, skinned and finely diced
Pinch of salt, 10 grinds of black pepper

Cram the nettles into a pan and pour boiling water over them. Cover the pan with a lid and simmer for 2–3 minutes. Drain the wilted nettles, cool, then chop them quite finely. Put the chopped nettles into a mixing bowl with the ricotta. Mix, adding the sieved flour, the egg yolks and 75g (3oz) of the parmesan, the salt and black

pepper. Mix all together thoroughly, then form into 12
oval-shaped gnudi.

To cook, bring a pan of water to the boil. Put in 4
gnudi and cook just until they float to the top, about 3–4
minutes. With a slotted spoon lift them out and onto a
tray. Cook the remaining gnudi in batches of four.

Melt the butter in a sauté pan, then add the salt,
black pepper, diced garlic and hazelnuts. Over moderate
heat, cook until the nuts are golden brown, but beware
burning the garlic because it will then taste bitter. This
will take 5–7 minutes. Then put the gnudi into the sauté
pan, carefully turning them over in the hazelnut garlic
butter. Before serving them on warmed plates, dust them
with the remaining 25g (1oz) of parmesan.

Nettle timbales

Serves 6
2 large handfuls of nettles
300ml (½ pint) single cream
3 large eggs and 1 large egg yolk
1 teaspoon salt, about 12–15 grinds of black pepper, a grating
    of nutmeg

Steam the nettles for 2–3 minutes until wilted. Cool,
then squeeze out any excess liquid. Whizz in a food
processor until smooth, then add the seasonings.

Whisk together the eggs and yolk, adding the single
cream. Mix the seasoned nettle puree thoroughly into
the egg and cream mixture.

Butter six ramekins. Divide the nettle mixture evenly
between the ramekins. Put them into a roasting tin and
pour boiling water into the roasting tin, to come halfway
up the sides of the ramekins. Cook in a moderate oven at
180°C (350°F, Gas 4) for 20–25 minutes, or until the
timbales feel firm. Take the roasting tin out of the oven
and leave to stand for 15 minutes. Then run a knife
around the inside of each ramekin, and shake them out
onto warmed plates. Serve either as a starter or as an
accompaniment to a main course.

Nettle and lemon soup

This is such a good soup. Thin and elegant, it makes a perfect light first course if the main course is rather rich and filling.

___

Serves 6
2 white onions, peeled, halved and diced
2 tablespoons olive or rapeseed oil
25g (1oz) butter
2 large handfuls of nettles
900ml (1½ pints) chicken or vegetable stock
Finely grated rind and juice of 1 lemon
1 teaspoon salt, about 10–12 grinds of black pepper

___

Heat the oil and melt the butter together in a saucepan. Fry the diced onions over moderate heat, stirring occasionally, for 8-10 minutes. They shouldn't turn colour but should look transparent. Add the stock, salt and pepper to the softened onions in the pan, raise the heat and bring the stock to simmer. Plunge the nettles into the simmering stock and bring back to simmer for 5 minutes. Take the pan off the heat, stir in the lemon rind and juice. Pulverise until very smooth, using a hand-held blender. Taste, add more salt and pepper if you think it is needed. Reheat, and serve.

Wild raspberries

Wild raspberries are, for me, one of the greatest of all edible treats. I once disgraced myself when judging a WRI jam competition by eating half the pot of one entry of wild raspberry jam. I just couldn't stop slowly eating the most wonderful jam I'd ever tasted! When you discover where wild raspberries grow, keep it to yourself and share the knowledge with no one else. Smaller than cultivated raspberries, and often misshapen, their taste surpasses that of any cultivated variety.

There are two ways to eat them – either just as they are, lightly dusted with caster sugar and with thick cream, or made into jam. But beware overboiling the jam – you want to keep the bright fresh flavour and colour.

Wild raspberry jam

Make the jam as soon after picking as possible – their pectin content is higher when newly picked.

Makes 2 precious pots.

900g (2lb) raspberries
900g (2lb) granulated or jam sugar

Heat the sugar. Put a saucer into the fridge to chill – for testing the jam for a set. Put two scrupulously clean jam jars into a low-temperature oven to heat through.

Put the raspberries into a large saucepan over moderate heat with 300ml (½ pint) water. Cook them gently until their juices run and the berries collapse. Then stir in the warmed sugar, stirring until you no longer feel grainy sugar beneath your wooden spoon. Then turn up the heat and boil fast for 10 minutes. Take the pan off the heat, dribble some onto the chilled saucer. After 2–3 minutes gently push the surface with your fingertip. If it wrinkles, you have achieved a set. Divide between the warmed jars. Put a disc of waxed paper on each, then cover each jar with cellophane. When cold, label the jars. And eat! Or store on a shelf in a cool place.

NB. If the jam doesn't wrinkle, re-boil for a further 5 minutes, after which time you definitely should have a set!

Rowanberries

Rowan trees have mystical properties. I would never cut down a rowan tree. But another reason for keeping rowan trees is that they produce wonderful orange berries in late summer/early autumn. These berries are very bitter, but they can be made into a clear, orange coloured jelly which is delicious eaten with game of all kinds. I include a couple of sweet eating apples with the rowanberries when I make this jelly. The apples just take the edge off the bitterness. And I find that half a cinnamon stick makes a complementary flavour to the jelly.

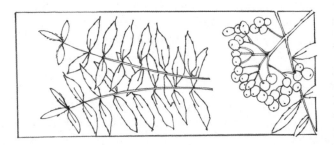

Rowanberry jelly

Makes 3–4 pots.

900g (2lb) rowanberries
2 eating apples, washed, quartered, but skin and core left in place
½ cinnamon stick
450g (1lb) granulated or preserving sugar for each 600ml (1 pint)
of strained liquid – you will probably need three times the
amount

Warm the sugar. Put four scrupulously clean jam jars into
a low-temperature oven to heat through. Put the berries,
quartered apples and cinnamon stick into a large
saucepan. Fill with cold water to come level with the top
of the berries. Put the pan on moderate heat and cook
until the berries collapse when pressed against the sides
of the pan with a wooden spoon. Take the pan off the
heat and cool the contents. Then strain through a fine-
meshed sieve lined with muslin, a tea cloth or J-cloth,
and collect the strained liquid in a measuring jug (you
may need more than one).

Put the strained liquid into a large, clean saucepan
and add 450g (1lb) warmed sugar for every 600ml
(1 pint) of liquid. Stir until you no longer feel any grains
of sugar beneath your spoon. Only then let the contents
of the pan come to a rolling boil. Boil fast for 10
minutes. Then take the chilled saucer from the fridge and

dribble a small amount from the pan onto it. Leave for 3–4 minutes, then gently push the surface with your fingertip. If it wrinkles, you have achieved a set. Divide the liquid between the heated jars. Cover each with a waxed paper disc, seal with cellophane and leave to cool. When cold, label the jars and store the rowanberry jelly on a shelf in a cool place, ideally a larder.

NB. If on testing there is no wrinkle, re-boil and boil fast for a further 5 minutes before taking the pan off the heat and testing again.

Sloes

Sloes are the berries of the blackthorn. They grow prolifically in hedgerows the length and breadth of the United Kingdom – but not in Skye, oddly.

Sloe gin

Sloe gin is particularly delicious! Here is how to make it
– although everyone has a slightly personal variation.
There are those who stick the berries – each one – with
nothing other than a silver fork. But of course, you can
stick the berries with anything which will pierce them!

500g (1lb) of sloes, each pricked and put into a large container
375g (¾lb) granulated sugar
1 litre (2 pints) gin

Add the sugar and gin to the pricked sloes. Mix well.
Store for 3–4 months, stirring or shaking (depending on
the container in which the sloe gin is being prepared)
every week during these months. Then strain the liquid
into bottles, after it has matured for 3–4 months.

NB. Damson gin is made in exactly the same way. I think
it benefits from 4 months' maturing.

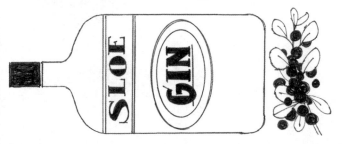

Sorrel

Common sorrel, with its pointy leaves, is a valuable food. It has a citrus taste verging on astringent, and is useful in sauces for fish and for chicken. Using half sorrel and half spinach, and with the addition of apple to the ingredients, an excellent soup can be made.

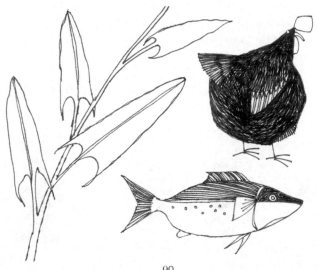

Sorrel hollandaise sauce

Serves 6, to serve with grilled or baked fish, or with roast chicken.

———————————

1 rounded tablespoon finely sliced sorrel leaves
3 large egg yolks
175g (6oz) butter, cut into 6 bits
1 level teaspoon salt, about 10 grinds of black pepper
1 tablespoon lemon juice

———————————

Put a saucepan about a third full of water on to heat until the water reaches a gentle simmer. Meanwhile, in a heatproof bowl whisk the yolks together. Add a piece of butter, the salt and black pepper, and put the bowl over the saucepan containing the very gently simmering water – the base of the bowl mustn't touch the water. Stir using a wire whisk, and add another bit of butter as the last melts into the yolk emulsion. When all the butter is incorporated and you have a thick golden sauce, add the lemon juice, mix in well, take the bowl off the pan and mix in the finely sliced sorrel leaves. Either serve the sauce now, or keep it warm but not on direct heat – a useful method for keeping any hollandaise warm is in a small thermos flask.

Sorrel, spinach and apple soup with turmeric

Serves 6

2 onions, peeled, halved and chopped
2–3 tablespoons olive or rapeseed oil
1 eating apple, quartered, cored, then chopped – skin and all
1 rounded teaspoon turmeric
220g (8oz) young spinach leaves
2 handfuls of sorrel leaves
900ml (1½ pints) chicken or vegetable stock
1 teaspoon salt, 12–15 grinds of black pepper

Heat the oil and fry the chopped onions over moderate heat for 8–10 minutes, stirring occasionally. The onions shouldn't turn colour, but they should look transparent. Stir in the turmeric, then the chopped apple. Add the stock, bring to simmering point, then add the spinach and sorrel. Bring the liquid back to simmer, and cook for 5–7 minutes. Stir in the salt and pepper, and whizz until smooth with a hand-held blender. Taste, add more salt and pepper if you think it is needed, then reheat before serving, but don't let the soup boil.

The Seashore

This, I feel, deserves to be a small section on its own. There is a vast number of items to be gathered on the seashore.

I find there are one or two ingredients which have become much featured on menus but which don't really deserve their place. Their flavour is almost a case of the emperor's new clothes. For me, sea buckthorn is the prime example!

But clams, cockles, kelp, mussels, razorfish and samphire – these are the things I look for and relish on my return home.

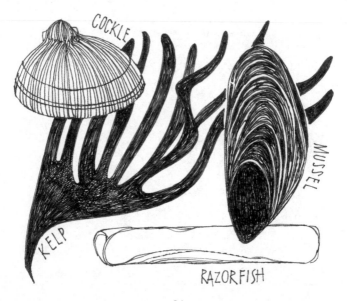

Clams with leeks, saffron and white wine

This is a delicious main course, accompanied by garlic bread and a mixed leaf salad.

Serves 6

2 kg (4½lb) clams, scrubbed
2 onions, peeled, halved and finely diced
6 leeks, trimmed of outer leaves and at either end, and finely sliced
50g (2oz) butter
1 tablespoon olive or rapeseed oil
4 medium-sized potatoes, peeled and diced thumbnail in size
2 generous pinches of saffron strands
600ml (1 pint) water
300ml (½ pint) dry and fruity white wine – I use a Sauvignon Blanc
1 teaspoon salt, 12–15 grinds of black pepper

Melt the butter and heat the oil together in a wide, large pan. Over moderate heat, fry the diced onions and finely sliced leeks together, stirring occasionally, for 7–10 minutes. The onions and leeks shouldn't turn colour, just soften and the onions become transparent. Halfway through this cooking time, add the diced potatoes. Stir in the salt and black pepper, and cover the contents of the pan closely with scrunched-up greaseproof paper or baking parchment. Cook gently for 10 minutes or until when you squish a bit of potato against the side of the pan it is soft. Then remove the paper, stir in the saffron,

water and wine, and add the clams. Cover the pan with
its lid, turn up the heat beneath the pan and cook for
5–7 minutes. The clams should have opened their shells.
Throw out any which remain closed.

To serve, ladle the clams and the leek and potato into
six warmed soup plates, and have a smaller plate at the
side of each person for salad and bread.

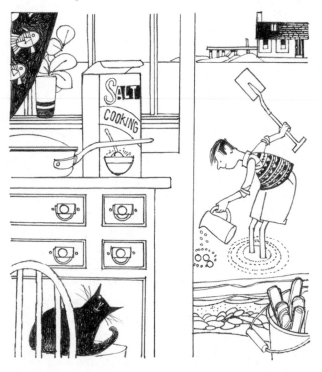

Cockles in tomato sauce with spaghetti

For this recipe you can substitute any member of the bivalve family – mussels, for example. Cockles grow in the sand, not on rocks. The same applies to them as to mussels and clams – having been scrubbed under running cold water, any which remain closed after cooking must be discarded. They were dead when picked. But those which are opened are so good stirred into cooked, drained spaghetti with the following tomato sauce.

Serves 6

900ml (1½ pints) cockles, scrubbed under running cold water to clean them before cooking
1 onion, peeled and quartered
150ml (¼ pint) dry white wine
600ml (1 pint) water

Put the cockles into a saucepan with the quartered onion, white wine and water. Cover the pan with its lid and cook, shaking the pan from time to time, for about 10 minutes from simmering the liquid. Take the pan off the heat, and pick out any cockles which have remained closed.

For the tomato sauce:
3 tablespoons olive oil
1 onion, peeled, halved and finely diced
2 sticks of celery, trimmed at either end and finely sliced
1 fat clove garlic, peeled and chopped finely
2 x 400g (14oz) tins chopped tomatoes
Finely grated rind of 1 lemon
1 teaspoon salt, about 12 grinds of black pepper
2 tablespoons of extra virgin olive oil

Heat the oil in a saucepan and fry the diced onion and sliced celery, stirring occasionally, until they are very soft, about 6–8 minutes. Don't let them turn colour. Then add the garlic, chopped tomatoes, lemon rind, salt and black pepper. Bring the sauce to a gentle simmer, the pan uncovered, and simmer for 5–7 minutes.

For 6 people, cook 450g (1lb) spaghetti in lots of boiling salted water until just tender. Drain immediately and mix the 2 tablespoons of extra virgin olive oil through the drained spaghetti.

Mix the tomato sauce and the olive-oiled spaghetti together, then mix in the cooked clams, discarding their cooking liquid. Serve in a huge bowl in the middle of the table for your guests to help themselves, or serve into individual warmed bowls, with a receptacle for discarded shells in the middle of the table.

Kelp

Kelp is identifiable because it is brownish-green, and grows in large leaves, sometimes with small bubbles near the base. I think of kelp as growing in the sea like a bush grows on land. Kelp is full of nutritional goodness – it is high in vitamin D, calcium and protein. Surprisingly, when washed under running cold water and sliced very finely, as in the following simple recipe, it doesn't taste salty, but instead tastes of the sea.

Kelp butter

This simple butter containing very finely sliced kelp is good served on baked or grilled fish of all types. You can steam mussels or razor fish and serve a generous few slices of kelp butter on each portion. This butter keeps in the fridge for 2–3 days.

175g (6oz) softened butter
1 tablespoon finely chopped parsley
1 tablespoon finely sliced kelp – well washed under running cold
    water, and patted dry with kitchen paper before slicing

Beat the butter and add the parsley and kelp, beating all together thoroughly. Put a large piece of cling film on a work surface. Put the kelp butter onto this in a fat sausage shape. Roll the cling film round the butter, continuing to form the sausage shape. Store in the fridge and, to serve, slice through the cling film into fat discs, peeling off the cling film from each disc before serving.

Mussels

Pick mussels from rocks which you know will be submerged by the sea at high tide. When possible, pick from rocks far from sand. This helps to make cleaning the mussels easier. When you cook mussels, always discard those which remain closed, never prise them open. If they remain closed when cooked it means that they were dead when picked. And the thing is that there is no way of knowing for how long they had been dead. Anyone who has eaten a bad mussel will tell you that it just isn't worth it! So leave and chuck out all closed mussels after cooking.

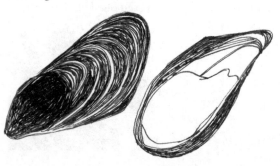

Mussel chowder

Serves 6, as a meal rather than a starter – this is a substantial chowder.

1.2 litres (2 pints) mussels, each scrubbed under running cold water
1 onion, peeled and quartered
150ml (¼ pint) dry white wine
900ml (1½ pints) water
75g (3oz) butter
4 onions, each peeled, halved and finely sliced
4 slices of best-quality back bacon, the rim of fat snipped off with
    scissors, the bacon cut into thin strips
450g (1lb) potatoes, peeled, halved and diced about 1cm in size
The liquid in which the mussels cooked – see method
1 teaspoon salt, about 12–15 grinds of black pepper
2 tablespoons finely chopped parsley

Put the cleaned mussels into a large saucepan with the quartered onion, white wine and water. Cover the pan with its lid, and cook on fairly high heat for 10–15 minutes, shaking the pan gently from time to time during the cooking. Check that most of the mussels have opened before taking the pan off the heat and cooling the contents. Strain off the cooking liquor from the pan and keep it for the chowder. When cool enough to handle without burning your fingers, remove the fish from the opened shells – if you like! This is not essential. Some people love shelling their own mussels.

To make the chowder, melt the butter in a large saucepan and fry the finely sliced onions and bacon strips over moderate heat, for 12–15 minutes. The onions shouldn't colour, but should look transparent. Then add the diced potatoes to the pan, stir in well, and cook, stirring occasionally, for 10 minutes, over a low to moderate heat. Then pour in the reserved mussel cooking liquor, stir in the salt and black pepper, and simmer very gently until when you press a bit of potato against the side of the pan it is soft.

Just before serving, add the mussels – in or out of their shells – to the contents of the pan, and stir in the chopped parsley. Serve, ladled into warmed soup plates. If you leave the mussels in their shells, have a large bowl on the table for the discarded shells as the mussels are eaten.

Mussels in tomato, chilli and avocado salsa

This makes an excellent main course for warm-weather eating. The absolute essential is that you discard any mussels whose shells remain closed after cooking. Leave a few mussels in their opened shells, as a garnish. Serve, if you like, with warm garlic bread.

Serves 6
2kg (4½lb) mussels
1 onion, quartered – skin and all
2 sticks of celery, broken
Small handful of parsley, stalks crushed

Put the scrubbed mussels into a large pan and add water to a depth of approximately 4cm (2in). Add the onion, celery and parsley. Cover the pan with its lid and put on a high heat. Cook for 5–7 minutes, shaking the covered pan once or twice during this time. Check that the mussels are opening. Take the pan off the heat, remove the lid and cool. Take the mussels out of their shells and put them into a bowl, but leave about six mussels in their shells. Throw away any unopened mussels.

For the tomato and avocado salsa:

It is so worth the small effort involved to remove the skins from the
    tomatoes.

12 ripe tomatoes

300ml (½ pint) tomato passata

1 teaspoon very finely chopped sweet onion – preferably from a
    white onion, but a red onion will do instead

4 avocados

Finely grated rind of 1 lime

2 tablespoons lime or lemon juice

3 tablespoons extra virgin olive oil

Grating of dried chilli (optional)

1 level teaspoon salt, about 10 grinds of black pepper

Assorted salad leaves, to surround the mussels in their salsa

Put a small pan of water on to boil. When it has reached
a rolling boil, stick a tomato on the end of a fork and
immerse it in the boiling water for a few seconds, until
the skin peels back from the fork tines. Lift it out of the
water and repeat with the rest of the tomatoes. Peel the
skin from the tomatoes. Cut each tomato in half and
carefully scoop away the seeds. With a sharp knife slice
each tomato into strips, then slice the other way, giving
diced tomato flesh about fingernail-size. Put the diced
tomato flesh into a bowl.

    Mix the passata and finely diced sweet onion into
the diced tomatoes. Add the grated chilli, salt and black
pepper. Cut each avocado in half, and flick out the
stones. Cut down the skins of the halved avocado, and

peel off the skins. Dice the avocado flesh into a bowl carefully – so as not to break up the diced avocado more than you can help – and mix in the grated lime rind and lime or lemon juice, and the olive oil.

Carefully combine the tomato mixture with the avocado mixture, adding the shelled mussels. Put this onto a serving plate. Surround with assorted salad leaves, and serve with warm garlic-buttered bread.

Mussels in creamy curry sauce

Serves 6
2kg (4½lb) mussels, scrubbed
1 onion, quartered, skin and all
2 sticks of celery, broken
Small bunch of parsley

Put the mussels into a large pan and add water to a depth of approximately 4cm (2in). Cover the pan with its lid, and cook on a high heat for 5–7 minutes. Lift the lid to check that the mussels have opened. Take the pan off the heat, remove the lid and cool the contents of the pan. Strain 300ml of the liquor from the pan for use in the sauce. Then remove the mussels from their shells, putting the mussels into a bowl. Be sure to throw out any unopened mussels.

For the sauce:
2 sweet white onions, peeled, halved and finely diced
50g (2oz) butter
1 rounded teaspoon medium curry powder
50g (2oz) plain flour
300ml (½ pint) of the strained liquid from the mussels' pan
450ml (¾ pint) milk
300ml (½ pint) double cream
1 teaspoon honey

1 tablespoon lemon juice
1 teaspoon salt, about 12–15 grinds of black pepper
2 tablespoons finely chopped parsley

Melt the butter and fry the onion over moderate heat,
stirring occasionally, for about 5 minutes. Then stir in the
curry powder and cook for a minute before stirring in
the flour. Cook for a further minute, then, stirring all the
time, add the cooking liquor from the mussels, the milk,
and finally the double cream – which must be double,
nothing less in fat content because then it won't thicken,
and could curdle. Stir until the sauce simmers gently. Stir
in the honey, lemon juice, salt and black pepper. Taste,
and add more salt or lemon juice if you think it is
needed.

Reheat the sauce before serving. I like to serve this
with boiled basmati rice containing toasted flaked
almonds and halved seedless black grapes. Not more than
5 minutes before serving, stir the shelled mussels through
the sauce, and the finely chopped parsley. If either sit for
any length of time in the heat of the sauce both will
deteriorate – in texture in the case of the mussels, and
colour in the case of the parsley.

Razor fish

The easiest way to procure razor fish (also known as razor clams) is to walk on the sands at low tide with a container of salt. When you see a little hole appear with a bubble, immediately pour a small amount of salt on it and the fish should pop up. My husband Godfrey used to collect razor fish with a spade, digging, at low tide. The one absolute about cooking razor fish is not to overcook them – they need the briefest cooking time. When overcooked they are like eating rubber, but when cooked properly they are exquisite eating. Best of all I like bacon with razor fish, although they are delicious eaten with a variety of other foods, including tomatoes, onions and nuts. But for me, the simplest is the best.

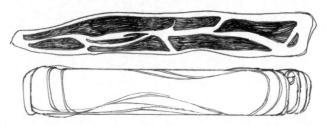

Razor fish and bacon

This is not an elegant dish, but it tastes so good! Cook the razor fish as soon as possible after collecting.

Serves 6

Approximately 900ml (1½ pints) razor fish, cleaned by washing under cold water

12 rashers streaky bacon – unsmoked – grilled until crisp

1 tablespoon olive or rapeseed oil

2 onions, peeled, halved and finely diced

2 tablespoons finely chopped parsley

Salt and black pepper to your taste

Cook the streaky bacon in a sauté pan. When crisp to your liking, remove the bacon to keep warm in a dish. Add the tablespoon of oil to the bacon fat in the pan and, on moderate heat, fry the onions until soft and transparent, about 8–10 minutes, stirring occasionally Add the razor fish, cover the pan with its lid and shake it over a moderately high heat for a couple of minutes until the shells open. Beware of over-cooking, as the fish will be like rubber. Add the finely chopped parsley and break up the bacon rashers into this mixture.

Serve, dividing the onion and bacon mixture between six warmed plates, and put the cooked razor fish at the side of each spoonful of bacon mixture.

Samphire

Samphire is a marsh grass, growing in salty water. It consists of vivid green stems with small branchlets breaking the straight stems. Samphire is very good simply cooked, as in the recipe below.

And can be included in all fish and shellfish dishes, where its presence contributes both flavour and texture as well as its bright, vivid green colour. But, whenever you cook it and however you use it, it's worth remembering that added salt is really not necessary – samphire is sufficiently salty itself for most palates.

Steamed samphire

Serves 4–6
500g (1lb) samphire
Extra virgin olive oil, or you can, if you prefer,
    use 50g (2oz) butter, melted
About 10 grinds of black pepper

Steam the samphire over simmering water in a covered container, for 2 minutes. Tip it into a warmed serving dish, and dress with extra virgin olive oil and black pepper – no salt will be necessary.